TOM

To: Sherica

Love, Tommy
9/30/2012

SOUL GRUB

SOUL-DREAMS PUBLISHING
2012

Copyright 2012

All Rights Reserved. No part of this book may be reproduced in any manner without the express written consent of the publisher, except in brief excerpts in critical reviews or articles. All inquiries should be addressed to:

Soul Dreams Publsihing
P. O. Box 153
Talking Rock, GA 30175.
www.soul-dreams.com

Published by Soul- Dreams Publishing Company
ISBN # 978-0-615-6249-7

Printed in the United States of America

Library of Congress
ISBN #978-0-615-62490-7

This book is not endorsed by Boy Scouts of America (BSA National)

Cover Photo: Dondi Fontenot—Dondiart Photography

Table of Contents

Introduction	6
Magic Pot	11
Appetizers	14
Breads	17
Stews/Soups	25
Breakfasts	37
Main Dishes	51
Side Dishes	77
Desserts	89
Boy Scout Specialties	98
Index	114

Introduction

We left at dawn after downing a quick trail breakfast. The sun was absolutely brilliant at this elevation. Nothing compares with a night under the stars, around 10,000 feet, in a high meadow; but we were up now and it was time to move higher. The summit of Mt. Baldy was our goal, with an elevation of 12,441. We would be there for lunch. We ate on the summit, in beautiful sunshine, finishing just as a storm rolled over us. Time to descend. Two hours later, we walked out of the hailstorm that we had been pounded with since we hit the tree line on our descent. Wow, what an adventure! Safely, back at camp just as darkness descended. It was "Time to Eat". Welcome to Soul Grub!

It is "Food for the Adventurer's Soul". I want to share with you a very unique cookbook. Many of my favorite recipes for feeding my own hungry self, but also for the many mouths I have fed over the years, are in here. More importantly, many of my favorite quotes, stories, and sayings gathered from over the years are also included in here. Enjoy each meal and each quote with a wide open mind and heart. Best served outdoors, but if you insist, try them indoors first.

It is my desire to introduce you to cooking in the outdoors, specifically cooking with Dutch ovens, but never forget that all of these delicious recipes can be cooked right at home in your very own kitchen oven. These recipes are tried and true for the home and the indoor oven, as well as, the outdoors and the Dutch oven. So, don't be scared of learning and trying out the Dutch oven. I give you the number of charcoal briquettes to reach desired heat, so go ahead and give it a try. It is fairly simple, just takes a little time, practice, and patience like anything else worth doing. Soon, you will be impressing all of your family, friends, and neighbors with your new outdoor cooking skills.

Furthermore, it is my desire to share with you my love of the outdoors, and the various activities that go along with that. My family has always enjoyed being and doing in the outdoors. Hope yours will, too. Something about the great outdoors that does feed the soul. It always seems refreshing to think of a favorite quote, saying, bible verse, or whatever your pleasure when standing on top of that mountain, or after finishing that exhilarating run, bike, paddling trip, or climb. Enjoy Soul Grub!

I believe Souls are being fed everyday. Are you in the audience, or are you in the game? Are you living the life intended for you? Soul Dreams start with one person.. You know, you are either receiving God's love or giving it. If it is your turn to receive, then relish the moment. If you are not, then you should be giving. Are you chasing your dreams? Are you doing for others? We should all be sharing something with someone that will make their life better than when you found them. I have always lived the philosophy that it is my personal responsibility to leave things one step better than I found them. In camping it's called the "leave no trace" principles. Leave the campsite better than you found it, with absolutely no signs of your having been there. That philosophy applies to relationships as well. Are you leaving people in your life better than when you found them?

Memories

The apron I gave her for Christmas last year was wrapped around her like a warm blanket on a cold night. The food stains and flour marks worn like badges of honor. The wafting aroma of cakes baking or biscuits or something wonderful to eat filling my senses. Those arms wrapping around me as if I were the most precious gift on that very special day. This is a constant memory of mine. I was very lucky. I had not one, but two grandmothers , and while they were very different; this scene was a constant scene in both of their houses. My first real memories are of food, lots of food, and the big white sheet that covered up the lunch meal when you were done. It would be there to snack on all afternoon, and then perhaps eat it again for supper.

Wham, the sound of that slamming screen door. We kids could not get out of the house fast enough. Our bellies were full, the air outside was cold. Our breath was frosty as it heaved in and out of our mouths. The cold was of no worry to us, we had trees to climb, privy bushes to hide in, rocks to skip, getting muddy, and just in general exploring those woods beyond the houses. Depending on our age through the years, we could be found on foot, go cart, horseback, or motorcycle, How far could I go and not get in some sort of trouble with Mom and Dad? Each day, each month, I was allowed a bit more room for "error'. I didn't realize at the time, it was just earned trust.

The stifling heat, the traffic, all the cars and people; growing up in the city, I could not wait to get to either our lake "house" or to one of my grandparents houses in the country. It seems as if every weekend we were at one or the other. We are a lake family. Growing up boating, skiing, fishing, we just in general love the water and the outdoors. Away from the city, we had no TV, water came from the well, no air conditioning, and most of the cooking was done outside. My love of camping came out of this environment. Additionally, my love of camping cooking came from these weekends. My friends, from the city, could never quite understand how we always ate such great meals and all the cooking was always done outside. Many of those early meals are found in the recipes in this book.

Of course, it was the adults doing the meals; we kids would just run up from the lake, soaking wet, and gobble down a meal only to run right back to the water's edge. There would then be more swimming, floating on those old black inner tubes, fishing with a cane pole, or anything else we might come up with. Occasionally, we would tie a rope around those inner tubes and try to hang onto it's slick surface while it was being towed behind the boat. Forget these modern day conveniences of handles and chairs on your tubes. We could water ski on anything that could float; paddles, sheet of plywood, chairs, over the years we gave them all a try.

My first canoe trip was across the lake, I paddled many miles and hours across it's glass surface. My favorite parts of the day are still sunrise and sunset, especially when there is water involved. Now, very quickly, I learned the value of the water moving and the faster it flows, well, the more I like it. After you have paddled all day and fought the river valiantly, there is something special about that Dutch oven meal or that cobbler dessert just bubbling over those hot coals.

Panting with my breath coming in short bursts, the hill before me seemed insurmountable. They said we were on a ten mile hike, but how far was that, and whoever said anything about these hills we are walking up. I was born in the flatlands near the water, but it was my Boy Scout troop that pulled the mountains out of my soul. Food always taste better, and the sleep is sweeter, when it comes after a good long day of hiking some of God's most beautiful mountains. Thirty-five plus years later and many hills climbed all over this country, I now know, that the mountains are the core of my soul, then covered with water, and basted in the outdoors. Sounds like a recipe of some sort. Enjoy Soul Grub. It is truly good for the soul!

My Cooking Journey

Learning to cook at a very young age, I was proud of the fact that I knew how to cook a real grits, scrambled eggs, and toast before most folks learn to tie their own shoes. You see, God blessed me with a working mother; and she made sure we knew how to cook that hot breakfast before we went off to school or on those days of school breaks. To this day, breakfast is one of my favorite meals to enjoy, especially if I am in my beloved outdoors.

As, I grew older, my ability to cook naturally grew. As those outdoor adventures grew, so did the experimentation of cooking in those same outdoors. I was no longer content to eat the same old camping cuisine. Truth be known, the real success came from us adult Scouters in our troop trying to out perform our older Scouts. We were always trying to "encourage" those boys by challenging them. As we began to eat better and better on camping trips, I began to bring the cooking indoors at my own house.

Having watched my grandmothers cook on their cast iron pans, it took a few years for me to begin to understand that cast iron pans, Dutch ovens, these types of cooking utensils.; they were all the same things I had grown up watching my grandmothers use. Our forefathers were cooking over wood fires, wood burning stoves, and using the "camping" products of today long before we in modern times discovered them at the local outfitter store.

Follow these easy to cook recipes and I will show you that you can enjoy cooking and eating in the outdoors as much as you do at home; however, you can also bring those cooking techniques right into your own backyard, up on your deck, or right into your own kitchen. Enjoy the book, recipes, and please share these techniques with your family and friends.

Here's to good eating, good friends, and good families.

Magic Pot

If you saw a late night infomercial discussing a "magic" cooking pot that would bake homemade biscuits, boil shrimp, cook a pork roast, cook breakfast, or anything else you could possible want to eat for a meal, chances are you would have your curiosity peaked.

What if this magic pot was non-stick, with a simple painless clean-up? Now, did you realize you could use this to cook a meal on your home stove, on your patio, in your fireplace, at your afternoon picnic, or on a family camp-out; additionally, it will be good for several generations to use.

This "magic" cooking pot is called a Dutch oven. They have already been used for many generations by Boy Scouts, adult campers, and real Cowboys working ranches. Most importantly, many grandparents of folks have used these "magic" pots for years. They have traveled to many "wild places", but have also been used in many homes, back yard BBQ's, and any place you can imagine. To some, it is an every day part of life already. To some, it is something they have used in the past. To some, it is truly a mystery.

I was making meals in ONE POT long before, I was a soccer Dad or Boy Scout leader. My desire is to enrich the experience of cooking for everyone. I am an outdoor cook, who learned to bring it indoors. I want to remind long time users of some different ways to use them and to teach beginners how easy and how "magic" these pots really are. Come and follow me for some delicious meals, you can cook indoors or outdoors. At home, on your back porch, or on that trip to your favorite mountain or river; you will learn to cook those delicious one pot meals we all crave. Enjoy this book for generations to come.

To Season or Not to Season

Dutch ovens are cast iron and thus very porous. Seasoning an oven creates a patina that keeps food from sticking to sides, bottom of the pot, thus making it much easier to clean. Additionally, the seasoning process helps keep the oven from rusting. A well seasoned oven will be black in color.

You can now purchase a pre-seasoned oven, however, I still recommend going thru the seasoning process before using or after a hard usage period. To season properly, place the oven and lid in the oven at 350 degrees and heat until very hot, then rub vegetable oil (not spray) all over inside and outside of oven. When it is coated very well, place on top shelf of oven and bake for one hour. It is then ready to go. Happy cooking!

Clean-up after Cooking

To clean your Dutch oven after use, use cold water and scrape off any food with a wooden spoon or spatula. If you have stubborn spots, boil water in the oven and this will usually take care of any problem areas. Do not use soap on your oven. After rinsing completely, re oil your oven and store somewhere dry and temperature controlled. Fireplace hearths make great storage spots and the cast iron pots are beautiful decorations.

Essentials for Outdoor Cooking

Dutch Oven	Cake Pan - 9 inch
Cast Iron Frying Pan	Round Cake Rack
Gloves	Shovel
Long-Handled Tongs	Whisk Broom

Baking Temperature Chart

* Courtesy of Lodge Manufacturing Co.

Desired Temperatures

Oven Size	325 Degrees	350 Degrees	375 Degrees	400 Degrees	425 Degrees
8 inch	15 coals 10/5 top/bottom	16 coals 11/5	11/6	17 coals 12/6	18 coals 13/6
10 inch	19 13/6	21 14/7	23 16/7	25 17/8	27 19/8
12 inch	23 16/7	25 17/8	27 18/9	29 19/10	31 21/10
14 inch	30 20/10	32 21/11	34 22/12	36 24/12	38 25/13
16 inch	34 22/12	36 24/12	38 24/14	40 27/13	42 28/14

SOUL GRUB

APPETIZERS

Real Men
Don't Cook
APPETIZERS

One Day At A Time

*A friend of mine was walking down a deserted Mexican beach at sunset. As he walked along, he began to see another man in the distance. As he grew nearer, he noticed that the local native kept leaning down, picking something up and throwing it out into the water. Time and time again he kept hurling things out into the ocean. As my friend approached even closer, he noticed that the man was picking up starfish that had been washed up on the beach and, one at a time, he was throwing them back into the water. My friend was puzzled. He approached the man and said, "Good evening, friend. I was wondering what you are doing."
"I'm throwing these starfish back into the ocean. You see, it's low tide right now and all of these starfish have been washed up onto the shore. If I don't throw them back into the sea, they'll die up here from lack of oxygen." "I understand," my friend replied, "but there must be thousands of starfish on this beach. You can't possibly get to all of them. There are simply too many. And don't you realize this is probably happening on hundreds of beaches all up and down this coast. Can't you see that you can't possibly make a difference?" The local native smiled, bent down and picked up yet another starfish, and as he threw it back into the sea, he replied, "Made a difference to that one!"*

-Author Unknown

There are hundreds of thousands of needs around the world. We can't reach them all, and even within our own groups we see our task overwhelming sometimes, not able to make any difference. However, to that one person or family who looked to you as a role model, a friend, an inspiration (even if he never told you) you've made a difference! That one action thing you do for someone can make a difference. Soul-Dreams is an organization based on sharing God's Love. Do your part today to be someone's action.

You Do Make A Difference -- in making our world a better place to be....One Step At A Time!

SOUL GRUB

BREADS
&
BISCUITS

Country Dutch Cornbread

2 cups of self-rising corn meal mix
1 1/2 cups milk
1/2 vegetable oil or melted shortening
1 egg, beaten
Pinch of salt

Grease a 9 inch round cake pan, preheated, then combine all ingredients, mixing well. Pour batter into a hot greased pan. Place pan on top of cake rack.

Bake at 450 degrees 20-25 minutes or until golden brown.

In 12 inch Dutch Oven,
21/22 coals on top
10/11 coals on bottom

Must we always teach our children with books? Let them look at the stars and the mountains above. Let them look at the waters and the trees and flowers on Earth. Then they will begin to think, and to think is the beginning of a real education.

-David Polis

Sourdough Biscuits

2-3 cups of flour
1 teaspoon salt
2 teaspoon baking powder
1 tablespoon sugar
1/2 cup melted butter
2 cups sourdough "starter"

Combine 2 cups of flour with salt, baking powder, and sugar. Pour "starter" into bowl, then add flour mixture and melted butter. Mixing well with a rubber spatula, add enough additional flour to make soft workable dough. Move to a floured surface and knead lightly. Roll dough about 1/2 inch thick and cut with desired size biscuit cutter. Place on a well greased cake pan. Place pan on top of a cake rack.

Bake at 425 degrees for 15-20 minutes.

In a 12 inch Dutch oven,
19/20 coals on top
10/12 coals on bottom

"There is more to life than increasing it's speed."

-Ghandi

Ice Box Rolls

2 packages yeast
2/3 cup Crisco
1 1/2 cup sugar
1 1/2 teaspoon. salt
6 cups flour
2 eggs
1 cup boiling water

Dissolve yeast in cup of lukewarm water. Blend sugar, salt, and Crisco (melting with cup of boiling water). Let cool and add dissolved yeast. Add flour and 2 eggs, mixing well. Knead down with additional flour and make into rolls. Place in greased 9 inch cake pan. Let rise until they double in size. Place pan on a cake rack.

Then Bake at 425 degrees for 10-15 minutes.

In 12 inch Dutch oven,
21/22 coals on top
10/12 coals on bottom

God is love. He didn't need us. But he wanted us. And that is the most amazing thing."

-Rick Warren

Sour Dough Bread

1/3 cup sugar
1/2 cup corn oil
1 tablespoon salt
1 1/2 cups warm water
6 cups of Pillsbury Bread Flour
1 cup "starter"

Mix all ingredients into a stiff batter.

Grease another large bowl (with corn oil), place dough mixture in and turn it over so oil side will be on top. Cover lightly with foil and let stand overnight (do not refrigerate). Next morning, punch down dough. Knead a little. Divide into 3 parts and knead each part on a floured surface a few times. Put into 3 greased loaf pans and brush with corn oil. Let rise for 4-5 hours or all day. Cover with waxed paper while rising. Place loaf pan on cake rack.

Bake at 350 degrees for 30-40 minutes.

In a 12 inch Dutch oven,
17/18 coals on top
8/10 coals on bottom

Then Jesus declared, "I am the bread of life. He who comes to me will never go hungry, and he who believes in me will never be thirsty."   *John 6:35*

Hoe-Cakes

1 cup of cornmeal
Pinch of salt
1 egg
Enough water to make a paste

Grease Dutch oven lid with vegetable oil, then place it over medium heat. Mix ingredients well, then pour out mixture like a pancake. Let it brown on bottom before flipping over.

You can not stay on the summit forever.
You have to come down anyway.
So why bother in the first place?
Just this:
What is above knows what is below.
But what is below does not know what if above.
One climbs, one sees, one descends. One sees no longer,
but one has seen.

-Terry and Renny Russell

Visit Us: www.soul-dreams.com

Join our Book Club to receive (10) extra recipes.

Monkey Bread

2 cans of biscuits (20)
1 1/2 tablespoon cinnamon
1/2 cup butter
1 cup sugar
1 cup brown sugar

Cut biscuits into 4 pieces. Place sugar and cinnamon in a plastic bag. Then place biscuit pieces a few at a time into bag and shake, coating them with mixture. Place coated pieces into a well greased pan. Bring brown sugar and butter to a boil in a frying pan then pour over top of biscuits in pan. Place pan on a cake rack.

Bake at 350 degrees for 35-40 minutes.

In a 12 in Dutch oven,
17/18 coals on top
8/10 coals on bottom

The words ``perseverance'' and stubbornness'' are not synonymous but it is distressing to observe that many people do not recognize the difference.

-Waite Phillips

CANDLES

Candle, candle, burning bright,
Just one candle for the night.
You will die before dawn's light,
By giving of yourself for another's sight.
People, people, scurrying through life,
To eternity you are but just one night.
Your dawn is breaking, where went the night,
Where went the light in your life's flight?
To curse the darkness or light a light,
Which is love, which is right?
Time spent kindly serving another's plight,
Will give happiness and purpose to your life.
Many candles burning through many nights,
Will turn many wrongs into many rights.
Oh what a world, oh what a sight,
All our candles burning with all that might!

-Francis E. Stein

There are many values in a burning candle. First, it needs the help of a friend to start it on its mission to serve others. Once lit, its flame burns upward and outward. Its flickering flame makes dancing shadows that mesmerize its viewers into a mood for silent reading, story telling, or imaginary dreaming. One candle offers little light and heat, but one candle can light another candle. The power, sight and feeling of many burning candles is awesome.

How many values for living can you find in the poem and the above paragraph? Where is your candle? Who is going to light it? What could your one candle do? What can many candles do? Probe your inner voice. Listen and heed, change an ideal into a deed, and light up the world! Finally, a candle gives its life for others. When your candle finally says "good night," will its light have made a difference in another's "sight."

-Love, Francis

SOUL GRUB

SOUPS
&
STEWS

Hoppin' John

1 lb. sausage
1 bag of frozen black eyed peas
2 lbs. rice
1 can of split pea w/ ham soup
Water
Pepper/Hot Sauce (optional)

Brown sausage in bottom of Dutch oven or pot. Boil rice in separate pot (10-15 minutes), salt and butter to taste. Boil the black eyed peas in separate pot (20-30 minutes). When rice is done, dump in the pot with the sausage, then pour the black eyed peas over the mixture (do not drain). Add the can of split pea w/ ham soup. Stir the mixture and let simmer over low heat for 10-15 minutes. Add water if needed. Add Pepper or hot sauce to taste (optional)

"If I have seen further than others, it is by standing upon the shoulders of giants"

.-Isaac Newton

Chicken Mull

1 stick butter
1 teaspoon salt
1 1/2 teaspoon. red pepper
Pepper to taste
1/2 teaspoon poultry seasoning
1 teaspoon worcestershire sauce
2 tablespoons vinegar
2 quarts milk
1 whole chicken
4 medium onions, chopped

Boil chicken in salted water until tender. Take the chicken out of the water and then remove chicken from bone. Chop or grind chicken. Then return chicken to water and add the rest of the ingredients. Let simmer on low heat til ready to eat.

Add crushed saltine crackers to make thick/mull consistency.

Those who know do not talk.
Those who talk do not know.
                                                -Lao-tzu

Irish Potato Soup

1/2 cup unsalted butter
1 teaspoon salt
1 medium onion, thinly sliced
1/4 teaspoon pepper
6 large baking potatoes, peeled and sliced
1 quart milk
3 (15 oz.) cans chicken broth
1 bag of frozen mixed vegetables
1/2 cup flour (or more to thicken)
Shredded cheddar cheese
Crumbled, cooked bacon
Fresh chives (optional)

Dice 3 potatoes, add onion, cover with water. Cook over medium heat until tender. Mix in butter, flour, milk, cook until thick.
Then cook 3 other potatoes until tender, then mash. Add chicken broth, mixed vegetables.
 Lastly, add your mixture from above into this.

Cook over medium heat until thoroughly heated. Top with cheese, bacon, chives (optional).

"Challenge is what makes men. It will be the end when men stop looking for new challenges."

- Sir Edmund Hillary

Santa Fe Soup

2 lbs of ground beef
1 medium onion, diced
2 packages of ranch dressing mix
2 packages of taco seasoning mix
2 cups of water
16 oz. kidney beans
16 oz. pinto beans
16 oz. black beans
1 frozen bag of white shoe peg corn
1 can of tomatoes

Brown ground beef, then add onions, simmer for 5 more minutes. Add ranch dressing mix and taco seasoning mix. Add water then add all beans, corn, and Tomatoes. Place all of this in Dutch oven or large pot and simmer for 2 hours.

Jesus replied: " 'Love the Lord your God with all your heart with all your soul and with all your mind. This is the first and greatest commandment.' And the second is like it: 'Love your neighbor as yourself.' All the Law and the Prophets hang on these two commandments."

Matthew 22: 37-40

Brown Stew and Potatoes

2 lbs of stew beef
6 Potatoes, peeled and diced
Small onion, diced
Vegetable oil
Salt to taste
Pepper to taste
Flour to thicken

Cut beef into bite size chunks then brown in bottom of pot with onions (in a little vegetable oil). Add water and potatoes, cooking until tender. Add salt and pepper to taste. Add flour to thicken.

Simmer for 10-15 minutes on low heat.

"We must view young people not as empty bottles to be filled but as candles to be lit"   -Robert H. Shaffer

Sweet Chili

1 lb. lean ground beef
1 teaspoon allspice
2 (32 oz.) cans stewed tomatoes
2 teaspoons salt
6 cups dry red or pinto beans
1/2 teaspoon hot sauce
1-2 cups honey (to taste)
1 teaspoon cloves
2 large yellow onion; diced
11/2 teaspoon pepper
1 lb. bacon; cubed
2 teaspoons cinnamon
8 cloves garlic; minced
2 tablespoons chili powder
HOT water to cover beans

Brown ground beef, then add beans, onion, garlic, uncooked bacon. Add enough HOT water to cover beans, then salt and pepper to taste. Cover and simmer until beans are tender adding additional water as necessary. Stir in tomatoes, honey, and remaining seasonings. Cover and continue to simmer for 1 hour.

Twenty years from now you will be more disappointed by the things that you didn't do than by the ones you did do. So throw off the bowlines. Sail away from the safe harbor. Catch the trade winds in your sails.
Explore. Dream. Discover.   *-Mark Twain*

Wagon Master Camp Stew

2-3 lb. boneless chuck roast
1 teaspoon sugar
6 medium potatoes, diced
1/2 cup flour
2 tablespoons worcestershire sauce
1 teaspoon salt
1/2 teaspoon paprika
1 teaspoon pepper
1/4 cup olive oil
1/2 teaspoon hot sauce
5 carrots; peeled & sliced
2 bay leaves
1 large onion; diced
1 teaspoon thyme
4 stalks celery; sliced
1 clove garlic; minced
1 quart hot water
1 lb. bag frozen corn
2 packets brown gravy mix
1 lb. bag frozen petite peas
1 packet mushroom gravy mix
1 lb. bag frozen green beans
15 oz. can kidney beans

Trim excess fat from meat and cut into 1" cubes. In a medium size bowl, combine flour, salt, and pepper and stir to mix. Add meat and mix until meat is well coated. In big pot or Dutch oven, over medium heat, add olive oil. Then brown meat on all sides.

Add onion and garlic and continue cooking until onions are soft and translucent. Add HOT water, gravy mixes, bay leaves, thyme, sugar, worcestershire sauce, paprika, and hot sauce. Stir to mix completely. Bring to a boil then add carrots and celery. Return to boil and let cook 15 minutes. Stir in remaining ingredients and bring contents to a boil. Cover Dutch oven and reduce heat.

Simmer for 30-45 minutes or until vegetables are soft.

"Somehow I can't believe there are many heights that can't be scaled by a man who knows the secret can be summarized in four Cs. They are curiosity, confidence, courage and constancy, and the greatest of these is confidence. When you believe a thing, believe it all the way. Have confidence in your ability to do it right. And work hard to do the best possible job." -Walt Disney

Jambalaya

Jambalaya Mix:
2 cups uncooked rice
2 tablespoon of instant minced onion
2 tablespoon of green pepper flakes
2 tablespoon dried parsley flakes
1 bay leaf
4 teaspoons beef bouillon granules
1 teaspoon garlic powder
1 teaspoon black pepper
1/2 teaspoon dried thyme
1/4 teaspoon dried crushed red pepper
1 cup chopped chicken (cooked)
1 cup chopped smoked sausage (cooked)

Bring Jambalaya Mix, 6 cups water, 2 (8 oz) tomato sauce to a boil. Mix in chicken and smoked sausage. Then cover and reduce heat. Simmer for about 20 minutes or until rice is tender. Remove bay leaf and discard.

Serves about 16 cups.

"The mountains are calling and I must go."

-John Muir

Visit Us: www.soul-dreams.com

Join our Book Club to receive (10) extra recipes.

Pasta Fagoli

1 28 oz can petite diced tomatoes
1/2 teaspoon extra virgin olive oil
2 cloves garlic, minced
1/2 - 3/4 teaspoon red pepper flakes
1/2 teaspoon oregano
1 cup diced celery
1 (19oz) can great northern white beans
Salt to taste
10 - 12 oz box of small shell or small elbow pasta

Sauté olive oil, red pepper flakes, oregano and celery, for about 10 minutes or until celery is tender. (be careful not to burn the pepper flakes.) Stirring occasionally., add tomatoes (don't drain) simmer on low for about 45 minutes. Add the beans (do not drain) and simmer for an additional 5 minutes

In a separate pot, boil pasta as directed and drain. Add pasta to the tomato-bean mixture. If you prefer it to be a little more soupy, don't add all the pasta. To make thicker add pasta.

"Nothing worthwhile was ever accomplished without the will to start, the enthusiasm to continue and, regardless of temporary obstacles, the persistence to complete."
-Waite Phillips

Rocks in a Jar

There is only so much a person can do. I have a real job (put rock in jar). I teach a Sunday School class (add a rock). I volunteer at school (add a rock) I run to stay in shape (add a rock) ... continue listing other main things you do. So, there, I'm full. I can't do anything else, even if someone asked. I expect most of you are the same way. You are so busy, you can't possibly take on anything else. Your jar is full also.

But, maybe if its not too big, I can do it. Like drive for a weekend campout, or arrange a fundraiser, or help at church one week, or plan a service project, or organize a parent's picnic. (add pebbles to the jar as you list the activities).

Wow, I guess I could do a little more than I thought. But, now, that's it, really. I couldn't possibly do more. Well, maybe if its just a small thing, I could. Like shoveling my neighbor's walk, or leading a game at a meeting, or helping someone with schoolwork, or cleaning the church for an hour. (pour the sand in as you list the items. Shake to settle).

Huh! Well, what do you know. Looks like I could do a bit more than I thought. I guess I just needed to make the time. As you can see, my jar is definitely full. I did more than I thought I could and I'm really able to accomplish a lot.

But, now I don't have time for just relaxing. How can I just have fun? There's no room left. (Pour water in as you list things). I want to watch TV, play video games, see a movie, play football.

The point is that you need to get the big rocks - the important things - scheduled into your life first. Decide what is most important to you and make time for it. Then, fill in your time with other worthwhile, meaningful activities. The time left over is your relaxing time. Be careful not to fill your life with the little things first or there won't be room for the big, important things.

SOUL GRUB

BREAKFAST

Coffee

One single bag of Instant Coffee
Water

Boil Water OUTSIDE of tent (backpacking stove)
Place single coffee bag into cup. Pour boiling water
over bag and let sit for 2-3 minutes.

Crawl out of your sleeping bag and it will be an
awesome day!

Ten Commandments of Human Relations.
*Speak to people - there is nothing as nice as a cheerful
word of greeting.*
*Smile at people - it takes sixty-five muscles to frown,
only fifteen to smile.*
*Call people by name - the sweetest music to anyone's ear is the
sound of their own name.*
*Be friendly and helpful - if you would have friends,
be friendly.*
*Be cordial - speak and act as if everything that
you do is a real pleasure.*
*Be genuinely interested in people - you can like
everybody if you try.*
Be generous with praise - cautious with criticism.
*Be considerate of the feelings of others - it
will be appreciated.*
*Be thoughtful of the opinions of others - there are three sides to a
controversy; yours, the other person's, and the right one.*
*Be alert to give service - what counts most in life
is what we do for others.*

Mountain Man Breakfast

1/2 lb bacon or sausage
1 medium onion
2 lbs of hash brown potatoes
1/2 lb. of grated cheese
1 dozen eggs
1 jar of salsa (optional)

Slice bacon and onion into small pieces, brown in bottom of Dutch oven until onions are clear. Stir in hash brown potatoes and cover; remove cover stirring occasionally until potatoes are brown (15-20 minutes). Mix the eggs in separate container, then pour over hash browns. Cover and cook until eggs start to set (10-15 minutes). Sprinkle grated cheese over eggs, cover and let cook until cheese is fully melted. Optional, pour salsa over mixture and cook another 5 minutes. Slice and serve like quiche (Real Men don't eat quiche, but we gets lots of requests to cook some Mountain Man).

In a 12 inch Dutch oven,
Place 12-15 coals on top
Place 8-10 coals on bottom

Good Homemade Grits

4 cups of water
1 cup of regular grits (not 1 minute or instant)
Salt
Butter
Grated cheese (optional)

Add water to pot. Add grits, tablespoon salt, spoonful of butter. Turn on heat, bring to a boil. Cover and turn heat off, allow to sit 5-8 minutes. Mix well.

Add cheese if desired

A few years ago, there was a wildlife organization out west that offered a bounty of $5000 for wolves captured alive.

Two friends, Sam and Jed, decided to make their fortune. Day and night, they scoured the mountains and forests looking for their valuable prey.

Exhausted one night, they fell asleep dreaming of their potential fortune.

Suddenly, Sam woke up a bit startled, and saw that they were surrounded by a huge pack of nearly 70 wolves with searing black eyes, and bared teeth. Low growls rumbling from their throats.

He slowly reached over and nudged his friend and said 'Jed, wake up! I think we're rich!'

Sam had a positive attitude. I hope you do.

Old Fashioned Oatmeal

2 cups of old fashioned slow cook oats
4 cups of water
Splash of milk
1 tablespoon Butter
1/2 cup sugar
1/2 teaspoon salt
Sprinkling of brown sugar

Add water to pot. Mix in oats and butter and sugar and salt. Bring to a boil, mix thoroughly. Turn off heat and cover. Let sit for 5 minutes. Mix in a splash of milk and a sprinkling of brown sugar.

Stir well and serve.

*"Some think that happiness comes from getting,
    Others know that it comes from giving."*   -Lord Baden -Powell

Sausage Balls

3 cups of Instant biscuit mix
10 oz of grated cheddar cheese
1 lb. sausage
1/3 cup of milk

Mix biscuit mix, sausage, grated cheese, milk. Roll into small balls. Place in a 9 inch cake pan. Place pan on a cake rack.

Bake at 350 degrees 20-30 minutes.

In a 12 inch Dutch oven,
15-18 coals on top
12-15 coals on bottom

Sausage/Eggs

1 lb sausage
1 dozen eggs
Grated cheddar cheese (optional

Brown sausage, drain. Mix eggs in separate bowl, then add to sausage. Over medium/high heat, scramble eggs/ sausage mixture until cooked. Add cheese (optional).

Can be served alone, with grits/oatmeal or in burrito form.

Everybody's Canoe

A young Indian brave was busy at work carving a canoe out of a log. As he worked, members of the tribe passed by. Everybody had a piece of advice to offer the young man.

"I think you are making your canoe too wide," one of them said. The young brave, wishing to show respect for the advice of an elder, narrowed down the canoe.

A little later, another warrior stopped by. "I'm afraid you are cutting the stern too full," he said. Again, the young brave listened to his elder and cut down the stern.

Very soon, yet another member of the tribe stopped, watched awhile, then said, "The bow is too sheer." The young brave accepted this advice as well and changed the line of the bow.

Finally the canoe was complete and the young brave launched it. As soon as it hit the water, it capsized.

Laboriously he hauled it back onto the beach. Then he found another log and began to work anew. Very soon, a member of his tribe stopped by to offer some advice, but this time the young brave was ready.

"See that canoe over there?" he asked, pointing to the useless craft on the beach. "That is everybody's canoe." Then he nodded at the work in progress. "This one," he said, is my canoe".

-Author Unknown

Are you listening too much to everyone else's advice on your life? Set your own pathway and follow your dreams.

Homemade Pancakes

2 cups flour
1 egg
1 cup of milk
1/4 cup of sugar
splash of vanilla
splash of cinnamon (optional)
1 tablespoon of vegetable oil

Mix all ingredients well. Heat skillet/griddle medium heat. Grease surface with vegetable oil. Spoon out mixture unto hot surface, sizing according to preference. When bubbles are gone on top, flip pancake over, cooking the other side.

Add Food Coloring for your favorite holiday!

Serve piping hot and smother in syrup of your choice.

How do you meet people's needs?
Love is the answer. God's Love, a love which is uncondi-tional, is exactly what the world and our community needs. Love isn't always popular, because love isn't easy. God's love is an ACTION. It requires you to get in the trenches, it required sacri-fice. It required perseverance and patience. It required putting others above yourself. I challenge you to both give love and ac-cept it. I believe as we all begin to walk in love, our families, communities, and world will be changed one person at a time.

-Kristi Overton Johnson

Chicken Fajita Omelets

12 eggs (3 per person)
Butter
Chicken Breasts
1 cup shredded cheese
Sour cream
Salsa

Cut chicken into bite size chunks, then cook in frying pan (with a little oil). In a small frying pan, place a small amount of butter. Heat until butter melts and begins to sizzle, then add 3 eggs, stir until yolks are mixed When egg is done enough to be flipped, flip it over. Place chicken on eggs, cover with cheese, sour cream, and salsa. Fold over and Serve.

"Following Christ has nothing to do with success as the world sees success. It has to do with love."   -Madeleine L'Engle

Orange Muffins

Navel Oranges (as many as you have folks)
Blueberry Muffin Mix (add water only type)
or any flavor you desire

Slice oranges in half, then eat the orange (to get your daily dose of vitamin C). Then clean out insides of orange completely. Mix muffin mix according to directions, then fill empty orange shell halves with muffin mix. Place in 9 inch cake pan, then place pan on a cake rack.

Bake for 350 for 20-25 minutes.

In a 12 inch Dutch oven,
17/18 coals on top
8/10 coals on bottom

A Candle

"The best candle is understanding."
"A candle lights others and consumes itself."
"Life is not the wick or the candle - it is the burning."
"Better to light one candle than curse the darkness."
"A candle-glow can pierce the darkness."

-Author Unknown

Dutch Oven JoJo Potatoes

1 lb bacon
1 medium onion, diced
8/10 potatoes
2 cups of grated cheddar cheese
Salt
Pepper
Small amount of vegetable oil

Fry bacon, drain. Cut into small pieces or crumble.
Sauté onions in small amount of cooking oil.
Add bacon, then add sliced potatoes (peeled or not).
Salt and Pepper to taste. Add cheese on top.

Bake for 30-40 minutes at 350 degrees.

In a 12 inch Dutch oven,
17/18 coals on top
8/10 coals on bottom

"I tell you the truth, he who believes has everlasting life. I am the bread of life. Your forefathers ate the manna in the desert, yet they died. But here is the bread that comes down from heaven, which a man may eat and not die. I am the living bread that came down from heaven. If anyone eats this bread, they will live forever."
                              John 6: 47-51

Real Homemade Biscuits

1 cup of flour
1 1/2 teaspoons baking powder
1 1/2 teaspoons sugar
Pinch of salt
1/2 cup butter
1/3 cup milk

Stir together flour, baking powder, and sugar. Cut in butter until mixture resembles coarse crumbs. Then, make a well in the middle and pour in milk. Knead on floured surface a few times (work dough as little as possible). Roll dough to 1/2 inch thickness and cut into 2 inch sections. Place in 9 inch cake pan. Place the pan on top of cake rack.

Bake at 450 degrees for 10-12 minutes.

In a 12 inch Dutch oven,
24/25 coals on top
14/15 coals on bottom

I expect to pass this way but once; any good therefore that I can do , or any kindness that I can show to any fellow creature. Let me do it now. Let me not defer or neglect it, for I shall not pass this way again.

-Etienne Griellet

Visit Us: www.soul-dreams.com

Join our Book Club to receive (10) extra recipes.

The Eagle and the Prairie Chickens

The Indian brave was walking by the cliffs when he stumbled across an eagle egg. He picked it up, turned his gaze upward, shook his head, and knew that he could not climb the cliff to return the egg to its nest. He searched until he found the nest of a prairie chicken and placed the egg in with the prairie chicken eggs. The eagle hatched and stayed on the ground with the prairie chickens scratching in the dirt for bugs and worms and seeds and never flying more than ten or fifteen feet, not knowing within its heart it had to ability to soar the skies. One day a mighty eagle was soaring the skies when the little eagle looked up and exclaimed, "Wow, what kind of bird is that!" The prairie chickens hollered out, "Shut up! That's the mighty eagle. You'll never be able to soar like that. Keep scratching in the dirt for bugs and worms and seeds." So the little eagle spent its life only flying a few feet from place to place on the ground as it scratched in the dirt for bugs and worms and seed with the rest of the prairie chickens. Finally, it died, not knowing that within it it had the ability to soar like the eagle, but lived its life listening to the prairie chickens around it, and all it did was scratch in the dirt for bugs and worms and seed .

How many times do we listen to the prairie chickens in our lives when within us we have the ability to soar with the eagles. We would like to be challenged and soar, but the prairie chickens say, "You can't soar. Be happy to scratch in the dirt for bugs and worms and seeds." They say you're dumb, you're stupid, you can't do that. We listen, turn our heads and thoughts back to the ground and scratch in the dirt for bugs and worms and seeds.

We as a people need to be pushed and challenge so that we can do the same for others. We must be careful not to be scratching in the dirt for bugs and worms and seeds, nor should we let our community scratch in the dirt for bugs and worms and seeds with they have within them the potential to soar, to fly as the mighty eagle.

SOUL GRUB

MAIN DISHES

Sweet Tea

Sweet Tea is First Main Part of a Meal

4 family size tea bags - caffeinated or decaf
1 1/2 cups of sugar
Water

Place 4 tea bags into pot of water and bring to a boil. Allow to cool down slightly. Put sugar in bottom of your pitcher, then pour tea into pitcher, add cold water over tea bags to top off. Makes a gallon.

For fun on a camping trip/picnic:
Place tea bags and sugar into a pitcher full of water and set out in the sun for the afternoon. Stir and pour over lots of ice.

"You shall love your neighbor as yourself."
Matthew 22:39

Pork Tenderloin

1 pork tenderloin
Salt
Pepper
Butter
1 cup of water

Pour 1 cup of water into baking dish or Dutch oven, then place tenderloin in oven or dish. Salt/pepper to taste. Cover in butter by rubbing it all over surface of pork. Bake covered.

Bake 350 degrees for 1 and 1/2 hour.

In a 12 Dutch oven,
17-18 coals on top
8-10 coals on bottom

"For God so loved the world that he gave his one and only son, that whosoever believes in him shall not perish, but have everlasting life."

John 3:16

River Runner Meatloaf

1 lb ground beef
2/3 cup dry bread crumbs
1 cup of milk
2 eggs, beaten
1/2 cup grated onion
1 teaspoon. salt
Pinch of pepper
Catsup
1/2 teaspoon sage
1/2 teaspoon thyme
1/2 teaspoon. rosemary

Soak bread crumbs in milk, then add meat, eggs, onion, and seasonings - mix well. Form into a loaf and place into an 8 inch oaf pan, spread catsup on top. Then place pan in Dutch oven on a cake rack.

Bake at 350 degrees for 45 minutes to 1 hour.

In a 12 inch Dutch oven,
17-18 coals on top
8-10 coals on bottom

The trouble with many of us is that we would rather be ruined by flattery and praise than saved by honest criticism.

-Waite Phillips

Low Country Boil

New red potatoes (about 4-6 per person)
Corn on the cob (small ears- 2-3 per person)
Kielbasa sausage (2 inch pieces - 4-6 per person)
Shrimp (about 1/2 lb per person)
1 Seafood Seasoning Mix

Boil water in deep fish cooker pot. Use enough water
to cover all food you are going to put in. Then add
seasoning mix, add potatoes (cook about 10 minutes),
add sausage (cook about 5 minutes), add corn (cook
about 5-10 minutes), add shrimp -cook until shrimp are
pink and floating. Remove from heat and drain all
water. Dig In and Eat!

*"No one should boast of being honest, dependable,
courteous, and considerate for those are fundamental
qualities essential to good character that everyone ought to de-
velop and use."*

-Waite Phillips

Beef Stroganoff

1 lb cooked roast beef, cut into strips
1/4 cup diced onion
2 cups water
1 large beef bouillon cube
1 10 oz. can cream of chicken soup
1 13 oz can mushroom stems and pieces (drained)
1 12 oz container sour cream
2 12 oz bag of egg noodles

Bring water, beef bouillon cube, onions, roast beef strips to a boil, then reduce heat and allow to simmer for 5 minutes. Stir in chicken soup, mushrooms, sour cream and allow to cook for 5 minutes. In separate pot, boil water and cook egg noodles for 10 minutes.

Serve meat over noodles.

"Seeing is a gift that comes with practice."

-Stephanie Mills

Deep Dish Pizza

2 packages of crescent rolls
2 lbs of ground beef
8 oz. cheddar cheese
1 can of pizza sauce
8 oz. mozzarella cheese
Pepperoni

Brown ground beef, drain. Remove your ground beef from Dutch oven, while placing 1 package of crescent rolls on bottom of 12 inch Dutch oven. Shred all cheese. Spread pizza sauce on crescent rolls, then add ground beef and pepperoni. Cover with all cheese. Then cover with second package of crescent rolls.

Bake about an hour at 350 degrees.

In a 12 inch Dutch oven,
15-18 coals on top
12-15 coals on bottom

"Don't overlook the obvious."

-Verna Reid

Mountain Top Chicken

4/5 chicken breasts
1/2 cup of sweet onion, diced
1/2 cup of red wine
1/2 cup cream of mushroom soup
1/2 cup cream of onion soup
1/2 cup cream of chicken soup
1/2 cup of sliced mushrooms (optional)

Sauté onion on Dutch Oven lid, then mix onion, wine, all soups and mushrooms in a separate bowl. Place chicken in 9 inch cake pan, then pour mixture over chicken. Place on cake rack.

Bake at 300 degrees for 1 hour.

In a 12 inch Dutch oven,
14/15 coals on top
5/6 coals on bottom

"It isn't important that we know where we are going or why we are going there. We only need to know the ONE we are following. The more we know Him, the more we love him and desire to go with him through the course He has prepared for us."

-Kristi Overton Johnson

SOUL WATER
www.soul-dreams.com

Did you know that the average American family uses 175 gallons of water per day?
Being one of our most precious resources, we need to ensure our water supply for generations to come.

All of the recipes in this book require water in some way or another. Let me ask you a question? If the faucet ,in your kitchen sink, ran dry; could you prepare a meal for your family?

Where does water come from?
Rain
Creek
Stream
River
Lake

Types of water purification methods:
Boil
Filtration System
Tablets
Easiest to use method is a gravity fed filtration system. Two inflatable bags connected by a filter system. Dirty water in bag on top. Gravity takes over. CLEAN water comes out into bottom bag. Pure, clean water to cook and feed your family.

What would you do without clean water?
To whom do you owe Thanks for your water?
What can you do to pay it forward?

Classic Chicken Pot Pie

1/3 cup of margarine/butter
1/2 teaspoon salt
1/3 cup chopped onion
1/4 teaspoon pepper
1/3 cup all purpose flour
1 1/2 cups chicken broth
2/3 cup skim milk
3 cups of shredded/cooked chicken
2 cups of frozen mixed vegetables (thawed)
2 unbaked pie crusts

Melt margarine over medium heat, then add chicken and onion, cook until tender. Stir in flour, salt, pepper. Mix well and gradually stir in broth and milk, cooking until bubbly and thickened - stirring constantly. Add mixed vegetables, then remove from heat. Spoon mixture into pie crust , then place 2nd crust on top, cut with slits.

Bake at 425 degrees for 30-40 minutes.

In a 12 inch Dutch oven,
18-20 coals on top
12-15 coals on bottom

Jesus said "I am the truth, the way, and the life. No one comes to the Father except through Me." John 14:6

Country Fried Steak

Cubed Steak
Flour
2 Eggs
1 cup milk
1 teaspoon salt
1 teaspoon pepper
Vegetable oil

Heat about 1 inch of vegetable oil medium high in Skillet or Dutch oven. Then, mix eggs, milk, salt, and pepper in bowl/dish. Dip steak pieces into mixture and then cover in flour (both sides). Place into hot oil. Fry approximately 6 minutes per side, flipping only once.

It is not the critic who counts, not the man who points out how the strong man stumbled or was the doer of deeds could have done better. The credit belongs to the man who is actually in the arena; whose face is marred by dust and sweat and blood; who strives valiantly, who errs, and comes short again and again -- who knows the great enthusiasms the great devotions; who spends himself in a worthy cause; who at best knows in the end the triumph of high achievement and at worst, if he fails, at least fails so greatly so that his place shall never be with those timid souls who know neither victory or defeat.

-Theodore Roosevelt

Chicken and Broccoli Couscous

3/4 chicken breasts - cut into bite size pieces
1 package frozen broccoli
1 box of couscous
splash of vegetable oil / cooking spray

Brown/Cook chicken in skillet over medium heat, make sure you grease pan before you cook chicken. Then in a separate pot add 1 1/2 cups of water. Dump in broccoli and steam approximately 15 minutes. In a separate pot, boil water (amounts on box directions) add couscous, cover and let sit. Fluff couscous. Add chicken and broccoli to couscous into the one pot and serve.

"The only things we keep permanently are those we give away".
-Waite Phillips

Pork Chops and Brown Rice

6-8 pork chops
2 tablespoons of vegetable oil
2 teaspoon salt
3 cups rice
1 large bouillon cube
4 1/2 cups of water
Pepper to taste

Brown pork chops in Dutch oven w/ vegetable oil, remove and season to taste w/ salt and pepper. Pour rice (not cooked) into drippings in bottom of Dutch oven, stirring constantly. Add Water and bouillon cube, then cook for 4-5 minutes. Add pork chops back in on top of rice and bake.

Bake 350 degrees for 1 hour.

In 12 inch Dutch oven,
17/18 coals on top
8/10 coals on bottom

"Never lose an opportunity of seeing anything that is beautiful, for beauty is God's handwriting -- a wayside sacrament. Welcome it in every fair face, in every fair sky, in every flower, and thank God for it as a cup of blessing."

-Ralph Waldo Emerson

Stuffed Hamburgers

2 lbs ground beef
Grated cheese
Onion soup mix
Cabbage
Catsup/BBQ/favorite sauce

Mix ground beef with pinch of soup mix, placing cheese in center. Wrap cabbage leaf around (may have to use toothpick to hold). Place directly in Dutch oven or baking dish.

Bake at 350 degrees for one hour.

In a 12 inch Dutch oven,
17/18 coals on top
8/10 coals on bottom

Always in a big woods when you leave familiar ground and step off into a new place there will be, along with the feelings of curiosity and excitement, a little nagging of dread. It is the ancient fear of the unknown, and it is your first bond with the wilderness you are going into. What you are doing is exploring. You are undertaking the first experience of our essential loneliness for nobody can discover the world for anyone else. It is only after we have discovered it for ourselves that it becomes a common ground and a bond, and we cease to be alone.

-Wendell Berry

Elephant Stew

1 elephant
Brown gravy
Salt and pepper to taste
2 rabbits

Cut elephant into bite size pieces (4 months)
Cook over kerosene heater (5 months)
Add salt and pepper

This will serve about 3800 people.

If more people are expected, then add two rabbits.
Do this only if absolutely necessary as most people do
not like to find hare in their stew.

Fried Chicken

Your favorite chicken parts
2 Eggs/ Milk/ Flour
Vegetable oil for frying

Mix eggs, milk, salt, pepper to taste
Dip chicken part in mixture, then coat in flour

Deep fry in grease (about 1 inch deep), medium/high
heat approx 6 minutes per side

Serve/Enjoy - I like to fry things outside!

The Bridge Builder

An old man traveling a long highway,
Came at the evening cold and gray,
To a chasm vast and deep and wide.
The old man crossed in the twilight dim,
The sullen stream held no fears for him;

But he turned when safe on the other side,
And built a bridge to span the tide.
"Old man," cried a fellow pilgrim near,
"You're wasting your time in building here.

"Your journey will end with the closing day;
"You never again will pass this way.
"You have crossed the chasm deep and wide,
"Why build you this bridge at even tide?"

The builder lifted his old gray head;
"Good friend, in the path I have come," he said.
"There followeth after me today,
"A youth whose feet must pass this way.

"This stream which has been as naught to me,
"To that fair-haired youth may a pitfall be;
"He, too, must cross in the twilight dim--
"Good friend, I am building this bridge for him."

-Author Unknown

Baked Chicken & Rice

4-6 chicken breasts
3 cups of rice
1 package of onion soup mix
1 can of chicken broth
1 can cream of chicken OR mushroom soup
Water

Pour rice (not cooked) in baking dish or Dutch oven, place chicken breasts on top of rice. Sprinkle onion soup mix on top. Pour on cans of chicken broth and cream of chicken OR mushroom soup then add 1 can of water for each can of soup. Cover with aluminum foil or Dutch oven lid.

Bake at 350 degrees for one hour.

In a 12 inch Dutch oven,
17/18 coals on top
8/10 coals on bottom

"A human being should be able to heal a wound, plan an expedition, order from a French menu, climb a mountain face, enjoy a ballet, balance accounts, roll a kayak, embolden a friend, tell a joke, laugh at himself, cooperate, act alone, sing a children's song, solve equations, throw a dog a stick, pitch manure, program a computer, cook a tasty meal, love heartily, fight efficiently, die gallantly. Specialization is for insects."
-Lew Hitchner

Dutch Oven Lasagna

4 lbs of ground beef
3 lbs of sausage
5 lbs of mozzarella cheese
2 large containers of cottage cheese
6 eggs
2 lbs of lasagna noodles
2 jars of spaghetti sauce

Boil lasagna noodles (only partially cook). Mix cottage cheese and eggs. Build lasagna in layers (meats, cheeses, noodles and repeat). Pour in spaghetti sauce and top off with remaining cheeses.

Cook 45 minutes at 325 degrees.

In a 12 inch Dutch oven,
15/16 coals on top
7/8 coals on bottom

Jesus answered, "Everyone who drinks this water will be thirsty again, but whoever drinks the water I give him will never thirst. Indeed, the water I give him will become to him a spring of water welling up to eternal life."

John 4:13-14

Cola Chicken

4-6 chicken breasts
1 can of cola
1 bottle of catsup

Mix catsup and cola, then place chicken breasts in Dutch oven. Pour mixture over chicken.

Bake 350 degrees for 30-45 minutes.

In a 12 inch Dutch oven,
17/18 coals on top
8/10 coals on bottom

When night ends...
"How can we determine the hour of dawn - when the night ends and the day begins?"
the rabbi asked of his students.
"When, from a distance, you can distinguish between a dog and a sheep?" one of his students suggested.
"No" the rabbi answered.
"Is it when you can distinguish between a fig tree and a grapevine?" another student asked.
"No" he replied.
"Please tell us the answer, then" said the students.

"It is when you can look into the face of a human being and have enough light to recognize in him your brother," the wise teacher replied.
"Until then, it is night, and the darkness is still with us."
                                                              -Author Unknown

Spaghetti Cheese Bake

2 lbs of ground beef, 1 med. onion
1/2 teaspoon basil, 1/2 teaspoon of oregano
1 (16 oz) can tomatoes, drained
1/2 teaspoon thyme, 1 garlic clove, minced
1 (6 oz) can of tomato paste
1 lb of spaghetti noodles
Salt and pepper to taste
1 cup grated parmesan cheese
1 cup of shredded mozzarella cheese
2 cups milk
3 eggs, beaten

Brown ground beef with onion, drain. Stir in tomatoes, paste, garlic, basil, oregano. Then add thyme, and let simmer for 15 minutes. Boil spaghetti noodles in salted water til tender. Drain noodles. Spread spaghetti noodles over a baking dish or in your Dutch oven. Sprinkle Parmesan cheese over noodles. Combine milk, eggs, salt, and pepper, then pour over noodles. Spread meat sauce over noodles, then sprinkle mozzarella cheese over meat sauce.

Bake at 375 degrees 40-45 minutes.

In a 12 inch Dutch oven,
18/20 coals on top
9/10 coals on bottom

Shepherd's Pie

1 lb. ground beef
Bag of frozen carrots
Salt and pepper to taste
Bag of frozen peas
1/2 cup of diced onions
Grated cheddar cheese
Water
1 tablespoon flour or cornstarch
Smashed Potatoes (garlic flavored optional)
1 clove garlic, minced (optional)
dash of garlic pepper (optional)

Brown the ground beef, drain. Add salt, pepper, onions
and let simmer for 5 minutes. Cover the contents with
water and simmer for a couple minutes. Thicken the
gravy mixture by adding (1 tablespoon of flour/
cornstarch with 1/4 cup cold water). Pour in baking
dish or directly into Dutch oven, then add frozen carrots,
add frozen peas and then add smashed potatoes (see
next recipe in book), then sprinkle with cheddar cheese.

"You miss 100 percent of the shots you never take."

-Wayne Gretsky

Smashed potatoes

1 lb potatoes cut into chunks
Butter and mayonnaise
Salt and pepper
Milk
Cheese (optional)

Boil potato chunks until tender, drain. Add butter, mayonnaise, salt, pepper , milk. Mash together. Place in a baking dish or cake pan (if using a Dutch oven). Spread grated cheese on top, if you like.

Bake at 350 degrees for 30 minutes.

In a 12 inch Dutch oven,
17/18 coals on top
8/10 coals on bottom

"Deeds are fruits, words are leaves." - English
"Good deeds are the best prayer." - Serbian
"Action is the proper fruit of knowledge." - English
"Better one living word than a hundred dead ones." - German

Visit Us: www.soul-dreams.com

Join our Book Club to receive (10) extra recipes.

Real Chicken and Dumplings

Dumplings:
2 cups sifted flour
1 teaspoon salt
Pepper to taste
1 egg, well beaten
3 tablespoons melted butter
2/3 cup whole milk
2 1/2 teaspoons baking powder

Chicken:
1 whole chicken
Salted water
1 stick butter
Salt/Pepper to taste

Boil chicken in salted water until tender. Then remove chicken from water and remove from bone. Dump chicken chunks back in water, add 1 stick butter and salt / pepper to taste. Bring back to boil.

Mix dry ingredients together:
Then add egg, melted butter, milk to make moist stiff batter. Drop teaspoons of this mixture into boiling broth. Cover well and cook for 18 minutes. Do not remove cover while dumplings are cooking or they will not be fluffy/light.

"Emergencies have always been necessary to progress. It was darkness which produced the lamp. It was fog which produced the compass. It was hunger that drove us to exploration. And it took us a Depression to teach us the real value of a job".
                                        -Victor Hugo

The Flashlight

Consider the flashlight.
Think how useful it is as we find our way along the trail at night
or prepare to bed down in our tents.

Consider the batteries in our flashlight.
If we keep them too long or use them too much eventually they
lose their power and our light dims beyond usefulness.

Consider that if we have only one flashlight for a group.
Then only the one person holding the light determines what we
will see or in what direction we will proceed. If we have many
lights, we have many possibilities and choices to make. Also
notice that if everyone holds his light high at the same time, the
light fills an area larger than if everyone holds their light low.
Notice how the group benefits from the light held high.

Consider what happens if we put our light inside a bag .
We can see what is inside the bag very well but can not see things
outside the bag. Sometimes it is important to see inside the bag.
sometimes it is important to see outside the bag.

The flashlight is like us, like people. We are most useful and
helpful to others when we are outside the bag and in groups.

The batteries are like our beliefs and our ideas. Sometimes they
need recharging or replacing in order for the light to remain
useful.

The bag represents some of the choices we make about sharing
our selves with others.
-Author Unknown

How will you hold your light? How long will your batteries last?
How many bags do you bring along and is there
 anything worth finding inside?

SOUL GRUB

SIDE DISHES

Calico Beans

1 lb ground beef	Bacon
Large onion	Salt
1/2 cup of catsup	Mustard
3/4 cup of light brown sugar	
30 oz. can pork and beans	
15 oz. can northern beans	
15 oz. can lima beans	
15 oz. can New Orleans style chili or kidney beans	

Brown ground beef and fry bacon, drain both. Then crumble bacon and mix with cooked ground beef. Mix in all beans. Add catsup, mustard, salt to taste. Add chopped onion. Place in baking dish or directly into your Dutch oven.

Bake at 300 degrees for 30-40 minutes.

In a 10 inch Dutch oven,
12-15 coals on top
10-12 coals on bottom

"Where the telescope ends the microscope begins. Which of the two has the grander view?"

-Victor Hugo

Corn Casserole

1 can cream style corn
1 can whole corn
1/2 box instant cornbread muffin mix
1 egg
1 cup cheddar cheese, shredded
4 tablespoons butter
1 onion, chopped
Salt and pepper to taste

Sauté onion and butter, Add corn, both cans (do not drain). Stir in egg and muffin mix. Salt and pepper to taste/ Mix well. Pour into baking dish or directly into your Dutch oven. Top with cheese

Bake at 375 degrees for about 30 minutes.

In a 10 inch Dutch oven,
15/16 coals on top
7/8 coals on bottom

Thou shouldst eat to live, not live to eat.

-Socrates

Macaroni & Cheese

4 cups of macaroni
4 eggs, beaten
1 cup of milk
1 teaspoon salt
Plenty of velveeta cheese
1 cup of bread crumbs
Pepper to taste
Butter

Cook macaroni noodles in boiling water with
1/2 teaspoon of salt until tender. In a separate bowl,
beat eggs then add milk and 1/2 teaspoon of salt. Pour
macaroni in 7-9 inch cake pan. Pour egg mixture over
this. Add lots of cheese on top. Put bread crumbs over
this. Place dots of butter on top of this. Pepper to taste
on top. Place cake pan into your Dutch oven on top of
cake rack or small rocks.

Bake 325 degrees 20-25 minutes.

In a 10 inch Dutch oven,
13/14 coals on top
6/7 coals on bottom

I can do all things thru Christ, who strengthens me.
Philippians 4:13

Grandma's Old Timey Rice

3 cups of Original Long Grain Rice
6 cups of water
4 tablespoons of butter
1 tablespoon salt (to taste)

Add rice, butter, salt to water. Bring mixture to a boil. Then, reduce heat to simmer for 15 minutes w/ pot Covered. Remove from heat, then allow to sit for 5-10 minutes.

"One doesn't discover new lands without consenting to lose sight of shore for a very long period of time."
                                                    -Andre Gide

Squash Casserole

2 lbs of squash
2 medium onions
3/4 stick of butter
2 eggs
2 cups crushed saltines
1 cup warm milk
1 cup grated cheddar cheese
Salt / Pepper to taste

Cook squash and onions together until soft, drain. Mash squash, onions, then add butter, eggs, salt and pepper. Soak crackers in milk, then add to mixture. Pour into greased baking dish or 9 inch cake pan. Put grated cheese on top of this. Place pan on cake rack.

Bake at 450 degrees until done, 10-15 minutes.

In a 10 inch Dutch oven,
21/22 coals on top
11/12 coals on bottom

"Make all you can. Save all you can. Give all you can."
-John Wesley

Sweet Potato Surprise

3 cups sweet potatoes: 1 cup of sugar
Cooked and mashed   1/2 teaspoon salt
2 1/2 tablespoon butter, melted 2 eggs, beaten
1/2 cup of milk   1 teaspoon vanilla

Topping:
2 1/2 tablespoons butter, melted
1 cup brown sugar
1/3 cup flour, plain
1 cup nuts, chopped

Mix all ingredients together and pour into greased baking dish or 9 inch cake pan

Mix all topping ingredients together and pour over potato mixture.

Bake at 350 degrees for about 35 minutes.

In a 12 Dutch oven,
17/18 coals on top
8/10 coals on bottom

"In preparing for battle, I have always found that plans are useless, but planning is indispensible."
                                        -Dwight D. Eisenhower

Awesome Baked Beans

1 lb ground beef
1/2 lb bacon
1 medium onion diced
1/2 cup brown sugar
1/2 cup catsup
16 oz. canned chili sauce
2 tablespoons mustard
1/2 lb precooked ham cubed
2 31oz cans of Pork n Beans

Brown ground beef, drain and remove to another Container. Cut bacon into 1 inch slices and fry. Add onions and sauté mixture, drain grease. Add back cooked ground beef, brown sugar, catsup, chili sauce, mustard. Simmer this for 15 minutes. Add ham and beans. Simmer for 2 hours over low heat.

"Be civil to all; social to many; familiar with few; friend to one; and enemy to none."

-Benjamin Franklin

Broccoli Casserole

1/2 cup of grated cheddar cheese to mix
1/2 cup of grated cheddar cheese to sprinkle on top
2 packages of frozen broccoli
1 can of mushroom soup
2 cups rice
1/2 stick butter
Salt / Pepper to taste
1 medium onion, diced

Boil 2 cups of rice with 4 cups of water, add butter,
Salt and pepper to taste. Brown onions in butter. Mix
all ingredients together with rice. Pour into baking dish
or directly into Dutch oven. Sprinkle cheese on top.

Bake at 325 degrees for 30 minutes.

In a 10 inch Dutch oven,
12/13 coals on top
7/8 coals on bottom

*"It is common sense to take a method and try it. If it fails, admit
it frankly and try something else. But above all try something."*
-Franklin D Roosevelt

Hot Pineapple Casserole

3/4 cup sugar
5 tablespoons all purpose flour
2 (20 oz) cans chunk pineapple, drained
1 1/2 cup grated cheddar cheese
1 stick butter
1 tube (36) round buttery crackers

Mix sugar and flour. Layer pineapples in a baking dish or directly into Dutch oven. Sprinkle sugar mixture over pineapple. Sprinkle cheese over this. Spread crackers over top. Melt butter, pour melted butter over top of crackers.

Bake at 350 degrees for 25 minutes.

In a 10 inch Dutch oven,
15/16 coals on top
7/8 coals on bottom

"A journey of a thousand miles begins with a single step."
-Lao-tzu

Visit Us: www.soul-dreams.com

Join our Book Club to receive (10) extra recipes.

Mashed Potatoes

8 potatoes
1 stick butter
1 cup milk
1 tablespoon of mayonnaise
Salt and pepper to taste
Cheese (optional)

Peel potatoes and cut into chunks. Boil potatoes until tender, then drain. Add butter, and milk a bit at a time, while mixing with a fork. Add salt, pepper, mayonnaise Serve as "chunky" or smashed potatoes.

Whip with mixer until smooth and then serve as "pretty" mashed potatoes.

"Being good is commendable, but when combined with doing good it's much more effective. A similar analysis lies in the fear of punishment for doing wrong instead of the recognition of benefits received for doing right. These viewpoints, it seems to me, represent the negative and positive thoughts of man."
-Waite Phillips

Climbing The Mountain

Afar in our dry southwestern country is an Indian village, and in the offing is a high mountain, towering up out of the desert. It is considered a great feat to climb this mountain. One day the Chief said; "Now boys you may all go today and try to climb the mountain. Start right after breakfast, and go each of you as far as you can. Then when you are tired, come back; but let each one bring me a twig from the place where he turned." Away they went full of hope each feeling that he surely could reach the top. But soon a fat, pudgy boy came slowly back, and in his hand he held out to the Chief a leaf of cactus. The Chief smiled and said, "My boy, you did not reach the foot of the mountain, you did not even get across the desert." Later, a second boy returned. He carried a twig of sagebrush. "Well," said the Chief, "You reached the mountain's foot but you did not climb upward." The next had a cottonwood spray. "Good", said the Chief, "You got up as far as the springs." Another came later with some buckthorn. The Chief smiled when he saw it and spoke thus: "You were climbing; you were up to the first slide rock." Late in the afternoon, one arrived with a cedar spray, and the old man said, "Well done. You went half way up." An hour afterward, one came with a switch of pine. To him the Chief said, "Good, you went to the third belt; you made it three quarters of the climb." The sun was low when the last returned. He was a tall, splendid boy of noble character. His hand was empty as he approached the Chief, but his countenance was radiant, and he said: "My father, there were no trees where I got to; there were no twigs, but I saw the shining sea." Now the old man's face glowed, too, as he said aloud and almost sang: "I knew it. When I looked on your face, I knew it. You have been to the top. You need no twigs for token. It is written in your eyes. My boy, you have felt the uplift, you have seen the glory of the mountain."   *-Author Unknown*

Keep this in mind, the rewards that are offered for attaining things are not "prizes." These are merely tokens of what you have done; they are mere twigs from the trail to show how high you climbed.

SOUL GRUB

DESSERTS

Homemade Ice Cream - Oreo

1 pint of whipping cream
1 tablespoon of vanilla
2 cans milk
4 eggs
1 cup of sugar
Whole milk
 Oreos (broken into chunks)

Mix eggs, sugar, whipping cream, and vanilla   Add
Eagle Brand milk and continue to mix very well.   Pour
into ice cream churn and add whole milk to fill line.
Add chunks of oreos (half sleeve or so to taste).

Churn until mixer stops or ice cream is firm.
Cover and let it set up.

Best if using a hand cranked ice cream churn on a hot
summer day.

*"Every day you make progress. Every step may be fruitful. Yet
there will stretch out before you an ever-lengthening, ever -
ascending, ever-improving path. You know you will never get to
the end of the journey. But this, so far from discouraging, only
adds to the joy and glory of the climb."*

-Sir Winston Churchill

Pineapple Upside Down Cake

1 box of vanilla cake mix
3 eggs
1/3 vegetable oil
1 can of pineapple rings
1 can of cherries

Mix cake mix and eggs and vegetable oil, blend thoroughly. Place a liner in bottom of Dutch oven. Place pineapple rings and cherries in bottom of Dutch oven. Pour in cake mix.

Bake at 350 degrees for one hour.

In a 12 inch Dutch oven,
15-18 coals on top
12-15 coals on bottom

Dump cake out! sometimes prettier than others, but always good eating!!

"Be true to your work, your work, and your friend."

-Henry David Thoreau

World's Best Pound Cake

2 Cups of plain flour
2 Cups of sugar
1 stick margarine
1/2 cup of block shortening
6 eggs
1 teaspoon vanilla
1 teaspoon lemon juice

Oil pan. Whip the shortening. Whip margarine into Crisco. Then add sugar, flour, eggs. Beat for 3 minutes.

Bake 350 degrees for 1 hour.

In a 12 inch Dutch oven,
15-18 coals on top
12-15 coals on bottom

By the time a man realizes that maybe his father was right, he usually has a son who thinks he's wrong.

-Charles Wadsworth

Black Skillet Chocolate Pudding

1 1/2 cups sugar
2 tablespoon flour or cornstarch
1/2 to 3/4 cup milk
3 tablespoon cocoa
2 eggs
1 teaspoon salt
1 tablespoon. vanilla
1/2 cup butter

Mix flour, half of sugar, cocoa, and salt (set aside). Then beat 2 eggs in a bowl (set aside). Combine milk, the other half of sugar, and butter. Pour this into cast iron skillet, allow butter to melt. Cook this slowly over low heat. Then, add dry ingredients. Mix. Then add eggs. Stir, Stir, Stir, Stir with whisk. Cook until thick and grainy. Pour into a bowl to serve with ice cream (optional) or just eat plain.

Opportunity is missed by most people because it is dressed in overalls and looks like work.

-Thomas A. Edison

Pecan Pie

1 cup of light syrup
1/2 cup of sugar
1/2 stick of butter/margarine
3 eggs
1 teaspoon vanilla
1 cup of pecans (shelled)
1 unbaked pie crust

Mix and whip all ingredients. Place unbaked pie crust into 9 inch cake pan. Pour mixture into unbaked pie crust. Place cake pan on a cake rack.

Bake 10 minutes at 400 degrees.
Bake another 35 minutes at 300 degrees.

In a 12 Dutch oven,
400 degrees - 19/20 coals on top, 10/12 coals on bottom
300 degrees - 14/15 coals on top, 6/8 coals on bottom

He who know others is wise
He who knows himself is enlightened.

-Lao-tzu

Derby Pie

1 cup of sugar
1/2 cup flour
1 cup of melted butter
1 cup chocolate chips
2 eggs
1/2 cup chopped nuts
1 teaspoon vanilla
1 unbaked pie crust

Mix sugar, flour, butter, eggs, vanilla. Whip this very well. Stir in nuts and chocolate chips. Mix very well. Place unbaked pie crust into 9 inch cake pan. Pour mixture into unbaked pie crust. Place pan on a cake rack.

Bake at 350 degrees for 45 minutes.

In 12 inch Dutch oven,
17/18 coals on top
8/10 coals on bottom

"Be a yardstick of quality. Some people aren't used to an environment where quality is expected."

-Steve Jobs

Homemade Brownies

1 1/2 cups flour
1 1/2 cups sugar
1 1/2 sticks butter
3 1/2 tablespoons powdered cocoa
3 eggs
1 teaspoon vanilla
1 cup nuts

Melt margarine, pour in cocoa, stirring. Pour in flour and sugar. Mix in eggs, one at a time. Add vanilla. Add nuts. Place in a 9 inch cake pan. Place pan on a cake rack.

Bake 300 degrees for 30-35 minutes.

In a 12 inch Dutch oven,
14/15 coals on top
5/6 coals on bottom

"Walking is the best exercise. Habituate yourself to walk very far."

-Thomas Jefferson

Visit Us: www.soul-dreams.com

Join our Book Club to receive (10) extra recipes.

S'mores

Box of Graham crackers
Large Marshmallows
Chocolate candy bars
coat hanger

Bend coat hanger making a long piece. Place marshmallow on end. Roast over fire (perfection is in the eye of the beholder). When done, place on top of one graham cracker. Then, add piece of chocolate candy bar. Top with another graham cracker.. Mash together. Enjoy. Repeat until folks are full or you run out of stuff.

"It does not mater how slowly you go, as long as you do not stop."

-Confucius

Mission of BSA

To prepare young people to make ethical choices over their lifetimes by instilling in them the values of the Scout Oath and Scout Law

Aims of Scouting

Citizenship Training
Character Development
Physical Fitness

Scout Oath

On my honor I will do my best
 to do my duty to God and my country
 to obey the Scout Law;
 to help other people at all times;
 and to keep myself physically strong,
 mentally awake, and morally straight.

Scout Laws

A Scout is:

Trustworthy	Obedient
Loyal	Cheerful
Helpful	Thrifty
Friendly	Brave
Courteous	Clean
Kind	Reverent

Scout Mottos

Cub Scouts "Do Your Best"
Boy Scouts "Be Prepared"

Scout Slogan

"Do a Good Turn Daily"

SOUL GRUB

BOY SCOUT SPECIALTIES

"For food, for rainment, for life, for opportunity, for friendship, and fellowship. We thank thee, O Lord"

"Philmont Grace", BSA

So the Boy Scout Oath begins

"On my honor, I will do my best, to do my duty, to God and my county; and to obey the Scout Law; to help other people at all times; to keep myself physically strong, mentally awake, and morally straight."

Their slogan is "Do a good turn daily" which means to look for ways to do an act of special kindness for someone else each and every day.

The Boy Scout Laws state that they are to be "trustworthy, loyal, helpful, friendly, courteous, kind, obedient, cheerful, thrift, brave, clean and reverent."

Not a bad set of guidelines for young boys or us. Have you ever noticed that they seem like an elaboration of the two greatest commandments and the fruit of the Spirit? The Boy Scouts of America have been around since 1910 and they have been helping to shape and mold young men for over 100 years now. The ideals still hold true today!

My own two sons are Eagle Scouts. They both participated in the Scouting program from Cub Scouts thru Boy Scouts. Having served along side of them as Scoutmaster for our troop, the memories and the bond are endless.

However, as I write this story, today is a big day for our younger Scout member in our family— my nephew.

He is a Cub Scout now. He watched and waited while his two big cousins did all of their fun Scouting stuff. But now it is his turn, and for him that means uniforms, badges, patches and…the Pinewood Derby!

Today is the big race! For all Cub Scouts and all former Cub Scouts, there is no other day.

Each scout begins with a block of pine, a set of four wheels and axles. Their task is to cut, sand, whittle, chisel, and detail it into their personal design. They have a specific weight limit they must meet (5 ounces) along with some other specifications. One week before the race is the "weigh-in" and if the car meets the specs, it is put in safekeeping until the big day, which was today.

My nephew's racer was named , the "eliminator". Unfortunately, it was "eliminated" by some very, very fast cars that were built by some of the older and more experienced Cub Scouts and their Dads.

So, this will be a learning year for him (and his dad!). . .
                                                    Continued

They examined the winners to see if we could pick up some tips and my guess is next year they will build an even faster pinewood racer. However, as I watched the Cub Scouts today and their parents, I had a sense that somehow this was how life in communities was meant to be lived. The boys were living up to their oath and motto. No bad language, no pouting for those whose cars didn't perform well, no quarrels or arguments. This was just a bunch of neat kids and neat parents and families all having a great time together.

Of course, there was food. The outdoor grill was burning, the hamburgers, hotdogs were sizzling. The side dishes, lovingly prepared, were being eaten. A very happy occasion.

Maybe we should have pinewood derby races for all the families in our communities. We could get together once a month to race our cars, eat, and of course share recipes. But, more importantly, to say "hey" and talk and laugh and, well, just be good neighbors to one another. We could call it the Pinewood Community Derby.

I suppose, though, we would all need to take the oath first like "love your neighbor as yourself".

I tell this story for all those who have the opportunity to share with our future generations the gift of the great outdoors, the gift of Scouting, the gift of good food and good recipes, and the gifts of our Heavenly Father.

Peach Cobbler

1 box of vanilla cake mix
3 cans of peaches
1 16 oz. Sprite

Dump cans of peaches into Dutch oven. Dump cake mix on top of peaches. Pour carbonated beverage into mixture, preferably of the lemon-lime flavor.

Bake at 350 degrees for about an hour .

In a 12 Dutch oven,
15-18 coals on top
12-15 coals on bottom

Apple Cobbler

One box of vanilla cake mix
3 cans of apples
1 16 oz. Sprite

Dump cans of apples into Dutch oven. Dump cake mix on top of apples. Pour carbonated beverage into mixture, preferably of the lemon-lime flavor.

Bake at 350 degrees for about an hour.

In a 12 inch Dutch Oven,
15-18 coals on top
12-15 coals on bottom

Philmont Hymn

*"Silver on the sage, Starlit skies above
Aspen covered hills, Country that i love
Philmont here's to thee, Scouting paradise
Out in God's country tonight
Wind and whispering pines, Eagles soaring high
Purple mountains rise, against and azure sky
Phimont here's to thee, scouting paradise
Out in God's country tonight"*

*These properties are donated and dedicated to the
Boy Scouts of America for the purpose of perpetuating
faith -- self reliance -- integrity -- freedom. Principles used to
build this great country by the American pioneer so that these
future citizens may through thoughtful adult guidance and by the
inspiration of nature visualize and form a code of living to dili-
gently maintain these high ideals and our proper
destiny.*

-Waite Phillips, December 31, 1941

During a very tumultuous time in our country, a Tulsa, Oklahoma
oilman led the country in a very generous philanthropic endeavor
for the Boy Scouts of America. He made a donation of land,
buildings, rental incomes, and cash that is still today the single
largest donation ever made to the Boy Scouts of America. While
I can not share exactly what was in Mr. Phillips mind at the time,
I have read and studied enough to know, that he believed and
supported the programs of the Boy Scouts of America. He also
appears to hold the same philosophy I share, one I learned from
Mr. Truett Cathy of Chick-fil-A fame. "It is easier to build boys,
than to mend men" The greatest generation was on the verge of
rising and the BSA was going to be in a position to lead. Thanks
to Mr. Waite Phillips. May we all be challenged to do our part.

104

Boy Scout "Easy" Corn Bread

1 Pack of Instant Cornbread Mix
1 Egg
Milk/Water
Aluminum Foil
4-5 small rocks

Place rocks in bottom of Dutch oven. Cover with aluminum foil. Mix cornbread mix with 1 egg and 1/3 cup of milk or water. Pour mixture onto aluminum foil like a cake mix.

Bake 400 degrees for 20-30 minutes.

In a 12 inch Dutch oven,
18/20 coals on top
10/12 coals on bottom

"I often think, when the sun goes down, the world is hidden by a big blanket from the light of heaven, but the stars are little holes pierced in that blanket by those who have done good deeds in this world. The stars are not all the same size: some are big, some are little, and some men have done small deeds but they have made their hole in the blanket by doing good before they go to heaven. Try to make your hole in the blanket by good work while you are on earth. It is something to be good, but it is far better to do good."

-Lord Baden- Powell

Breakfast Burritos

Tortillas
1 lb. sausage and / or bacon
1 dozen eggs
grated cheese

Brown sausage in pan, drain. Cook bacon in separate pan, allow to cool and break into small pieces. Mix eggs in separate bowl. Add eggs into sausage/bacon mixture, scrambling as they cook. Add grated cheese to taste. Place a spoonful inside a tortilla and roll up.

Boy Scout "Womp" Biscuits

1 Can of Biscuits (whatever type you desire)
Aluminum Foil
5-6 small rocks

Place rocks in bottom of Dutch oven. Cover rocks and sides with aluminum foil. Place biscuits on top of aluminum foil.

Bake at 350 degrees 15 -20 minutes.

In a 12 inch Dutch oven,
17/18 coals on top
8/10 coals on bottom

Brunswick Stew

2 lbs. ground beef
3 cans of chicken (4-6 oz.)
1 lb. BBQ pork (cooked/canned)
2 cans of corn (I prefer white/cream style corn)
1 bottle of catsup
32 oz. or water
Hot Sauce (optional)

Brown ground beef in bottom of Dutch oven, drain.
Dump in chicken. Dump in bbq pork. Dump in cans of
corn. Dump in bottle catsup. Add 32 oz. of water
Let simmer for 15-20 minutes. Add hot sauce to taste
(optional). Longer it simmers, the better it is.

*"Put a boy in touch with nature and the job of inspiring him
with high ideals is an easier one than in any other
environment."*
                                                    -Waite Phillips

Chicken 'n Dumplings

Feeds 8 people:
4 cans of biscuits (cheaper the better)
Flour (enough to mix biscuits in)
4 cans of chicken (4-6 oz.)
Seasoning salt
Corn starch
Water

Boil water in Large Dutch oven /Pot. Add seasoning salt to taste. While waiting on water to boil, cut/tear biscuits into sections of four. Put flour in a bowl, mix biscuit pieces into flour. After water boils, add biscuits coated in flour into water. Let cook 10-15 minutes Add chicken. Add flour to thicken mixture

Spaghetti for a Crowd Quickly

1 lb. ground beef
1 lb of sausage
2 jars of meat flavored spaghetti sauce
1 teaspoon of garlic salt
1 teaspoon of pepper
2 lbs of spaghetti noodles

Brown ground beef and sausage, drain grease. Add spaghetti sauce. Add garlic salt , pepper. Mix well, let simmer on low heat. Boil pot of water. Break noodles in half and place in water. Boil 15-20 minutes. Strain water off noodles.

Serve separately or combine in one pot and serve.

Chicken and Rice

2 lb box of rice
20 oz. of chicken - cans
2 cans of mixed vegetables

Boil water (amounts per instructions). Add Rice, Let cook 15 minutes. Add chicken. Add vegetables. Allow to simmer 5 - 10 minutes.

"Real philanthropy consists of helping others, outside our own family circle, from whom no thanks is expected or required. "
-Waite Phillips

BBQ Chicken or Salsa Chicken

Chicken Breasts (cut into small pieces)
Bottle of BBQ sauce
or
Bottle salsa

Grease skillet. Cook/ chicken breast pieces over medium heat. Add BBQ sauce or salsa

Mix well and allow to simmer over low heat

Be prepared

There is no religious side of the movement; the whole of it is based upon religion.

As a Scout, you are obliged to do at least one good turn every day.

You can smile at the rain if you have pitched your tent properly.

Scouts learn endurances in the open. Like explorers, they carry their own burdens and 'paddle their own canoes.'

A scout is 'clean in thought, word and deed.'

A boy learning what he can as a scout, has a good chance in the world.

-BSA Collection

No Drip Tacos

2 lbs of ground beef
2 10 oz cans of tomato soup
2 cans of canned tomatoes
2 cans of ranch-style beans
1 or 2 dashes of hot sauce (optional)
Lettuce - shredded (optional)
Cheese - grated (optional)

Brown ground beef and drain. Add tomato soup, canned tomatoes, beans, and hot sauce, and simmer for about 20 minutes. Spoon mixture over corn chips or broken taco chips. Top with lettuce, grated cheese if desired.

Most Boy Scouts use individual bags of Frito's and eat straight from bag. No clean up.

Good Deeds

How many good deed examples can you give that impacted the world?

"This I believe: A hundred years from now it will not matter what my bank account was, the sort of house I lived in, or the kind of car I drove. But the world may be different because I was important in the life of a boy."

-Author Unknown

Coffee Can Stew

Coffee Can
Bacon (uncooked)
Meatballs (ground beef, turkey, pre-made)
Beef Stew Meat
Diced Chicken
Diced Potatoes
Diced Carrots
Diced Onions
Salt/Pepper to taste
Water

Layer the bottom of the coffee can with bacon, then add meat, vegetables, meat, vegetables until 3/4 full. Add salt and pepper. Add about 1 and 1/2 cups of water. Place can in a bed of coals and cover top with foil. Let cook for about an hour. No peeking. Use oven mitts to remove from heat and serve from can.

"To see is one of God's greatest gifts to man and to comprehend what we see doubly so. Furthermore, he has endowed some people with the qualities to see the beauties of life and nature much more than others and they have the greatest gift of all. "
-Waite Phillips

Camping Doughnuts

Canned Biscuits (the cheaper the better)
Sugar
Cinnamon
Vegetable Oil

Put vegetable oil in your Dutch oven, heat up
Punch a hole in your biscuits and drop in hot oil
Let cool and roll in sugar and cinnamon mix.

Keep cooking until everyone in camp is happy!!!

Cardboard Box Cookies

Cardboard Box
Coat Hangers
Aluminum Foil
Slice/Bake Cookies

Cover your box with aluminum foil, even lid.
Run your coat hangers thru sides of box creating a rack.
Cut the bottom off of your box, but have lid opening for
access to your cookies. Place over coals and add
cookies. You can use a cake pan of sorts or line cookies
on aluminum foil sheet and lift in and out of "oven".
You will be the HIT of any Cub Scout function, I assure
you. Cook until kids are ready for bed or you run out of
cookies.

The Last Letter

Dear Scouts,

If you have ever seen the play Peter Pan you will remember how the pirate chief was always making his dying speech because he was afraid that possibly when the time came for him to die he might not have time to get it off his chest. It is much the same with me, and so, although I am not at this moment dying, I shall be doing so one of these days and I want to send you a parting word of good-bye.

I have had a most happy life and I want each one of you to have as happy a life too. I believe that God put us in this jolly world to be happy and enjoy life. Happiness doesn't come from being rich, nor merely from being successful in your career, nor by self-indulgence. One step towards happiness is to make yourself healthy and strong while you are a boy, so that you can be useful and so can enjoy life when you are a man.

Nature study will show you how full of beautiful and wonderful things God has made the world for you to enjoy. Be contented with what you have got and make the best of it. Look on the bright side of things instead of the gloomy one.
But the real way to get happiness is by giving out happiness to other people. Try and leave this world a little better than you found it and when your turn comes to die, you can die happy in feeling that at any rate you have not wasted your time but have done your best.

"Be Prepared" in this way, to live happy and to die happy - stick to your Scout promise always - even after you have ceased to be a boy - and God help you to do it.

Your Friend,
Lord Baden -Powell.

Ya GoddaWanna

In the great Northwest where I grew up, I met a mountain man and he knew how to get many things done with very little resources. He had almost nothing to work with, but accomplished great things. Whether the task was to build a fire underwater or stop a waterfall from falling, it seemed he could take care of it. I was so amazed to see the things he could do, I finally asked him how he did it.

He told me that a long time ago, he had found a magical solution to nearly all challenges that came along. He said it was all contained in a single, ancient word that had mystic powers. When you understand the meaning of the word, it unleashes immense strength and abilities; it makes your mind more clear; it makes your imagination run wild with ideas.

Well, of course, I could hardly contain myself and I just had to know what this powerful magic was. I pleaded with him to tell me and he finally agreed.

He said the word is, 'YAGODDAWANNA'.

In order to accomplish anything, whether it is small or big, easy or difficult, trivial or of utmost importance, in order to be successful, you've got to want to do it. To earn good grades, you gotta wanna earn them. To become an Eagle Scout, ya godda wanna be one. The main reason people don't succeed at something is because they don't really want it bad enough. By really wanting something, you come up with ideas, make plans, and then do it.

It is my hope that you enjoyed this Soul Grub. I hope you fed the belly and fed the soul, now go out and spread God's Love in your way in your family, and in your community.

Remember, to do something YaGoddaWanna do it.

Index

Breads & Biscuits

Country Dutch Cornbread	18
Hoe Cakes	22
Ice Box Rolls	20
Monkey Bread	23
Sourdough Biscuits	19
Sourdough Bread	21

Soup & Stews

Brown Stew and Potatoes	30
Chicken Mull	27
Hoppin' John	26
Irish Potato Soup	28
Jambalaya	34
Pasta Fajoli	35
Santa Fe Soup	29
Sweet Chili	31
Wagon Master Stew	32

Breakfast

Coffee	38
Chicken Fajita Omelets	45
Good Homemade Grits	40
Homemade Pancakes	44
JoJo Dutch Oven Potatoes	47
Mountain Man Breakfast	39
Old Fashioned Oatmeal	41
Orange Muffins	46
Real Homemade Biscuits	48
Sausage Balls	42
Sausage / Eggs	42

Side Dishes

Awesome Baked Beans	84
Broccoli Casserole	85
Calico Beans	78
Corn Casserole	79
Grandma's Old Timey Rice	81
Hot Pineapple Casserole	86
Macaroni & Cheese	80
Mashed Potatoes	87
Squash Casserole	82
Sweet Potato Surprise	83

Main Dishes

Baked Chicken and Rice	69
Beef Stroganoff	56
Chicken and Broccoli Couscous	64
Classic Chicken Pot Pie	62
Coca Cola Chicken	71
Country Fried Steak	63
Deep Dish Pizza	57
Dutch Oven Lasagna	70
Elephant Stew	67
Fried Chicken	67
Low Country Boil	55
Mountain Top Chicken	58
Pork Chops and Brown Rice	65
Pork Tenderloin	53
Real Chicken & Dumplings	75
Shepherd's Pie	73
Smashed Potatoes	72
Spaghetti Cheese Bake	72
Stuffed Hamburgers	66
Sweet Tea	52

Desserts

Black Skillet Chocolate Pudding	93
Derby Pie	95
Homemade Brownies	90
Homemade Ice Cream	96
Pecan Pie	94
Pineapple Upside Down Cake	91
S'mores	97
World's Best Pound Cake	92

Boy Scout Specialties

Apple Cobbler	103
BBQ Chicken	110
Breakfast Burritos	106
Boy Scout "Easy" Cornbread	105
Boy Scout "Womp" Biscuits	106
Brunswick Stew	107
Chicken & Dumplings	108
Chicken & Rice	109
No Drip Tacos	111
Peach Cobbler	103
Spaghetti for a Crowd	109

Quotations

Confucious	97
Lord Baden-Powell	41, 105, 112
Wendell Berry	66
Sir Winston Churchill	90
Walt Disney	33
Thomas Edison	93
Dwight D. Eisenhower	83
Ralph Waldo Emerson	65
Benjamin Franklin	84
Ghandi	19
Andre Gide	81
Wayne Gretsky	73
Etienne Griellet	48
Sir Edmund Hillary	28
Lew Hitchner	69
Victor Hugo	75, 78
Thomas Jefferson	96
Steve Jobs	95
Kristi Overton Johnson	44, 58
Lao-tzu	27, 79, 94
Madeleine L'Engle	45
Stephanie Mills	56
John Muir	34
Isaac Newton	26
Waite Phillips	23, 35, 54, 55, 64, 87, 104, 107, 109, 112
David Polis	18
Verna Reid	57
Franklin Delano Roosevelt	85
Theodore Roosevelt	63
Terry & Renny Russell	22
Robert H. Shaffer	30
Francis E. Stein	24
Socrates	79
Henry David Thoreau	91
Mark Twain	31
Charles Wadsworth	92
Rick Warren	20
John Wesley	82

HOW TO ORDER

Order additional copies of this cookbook as an ideal gift for family and friends.

Send check or money order along with order form below to:

Soul Dreams Publishing
P. O. Box 153
Talking Rock, GA 30175

OR

Order online

www.soul-dreams.com

sales @soul-dreams.com

Please send me _____ copies of **Soul Grub** at $14.95 each, plus $2.50 shipping and handling per book ordered.

Mail books to :

Name _____
Address _____
City _____
State _____
Zip _____
Email _____

SHARE WITH US

Join our Soul Dreams Club!
Visit our website for (10) extra recipes
www.soul-dreams.com

Soul Dreams hopes you enjoy this cook book. We truly
hope you accept the challenges.

Go for a walk.
Go for a run.
Go for a hike.
Paddle a River.
Climb a rock face.
Backpack a trail.
Go snow skiing.
Go water skiing.
Ride your bike.
Go camping.
Build a campfire.
Get involved

Protect the outdoors!

Send us an email of your adventures and your
adventure cooking.
Send us your story of your Soul Dreams.

info@soul-dreams.com

Visit Us: www.soul-dreams.com

SOUL WATER

RESTORING BODY, MIND, AND HOPE

By: Tom Roberson

Chapter 1

Water!

It is a beautiful afternoon sometime in late June in 2007. I am with a group backpacking in the Sangre de Cristos Mountains in northern New Mexico. Here we are, climbing Mt. Phillips.

Located at the Philmont Scout Ranch in Cimarron, NM, Mt. Phillips is over 12,000 feet in elevation and we are sleeping on the summit tonight. Eight Days into a backpacking trek, in the summer heat at elevation, I could not get enough water to drink. The temperature is about 85 degrees currently with sun shining brightly. Our schedule calls for a dry camp tonight. What exactly is a dry camp?

It means exactly what it appears. Dry, as in zero, none, no water for tonight at our campsite. Great, so now we were facing a 2,000 climb and an overnight stay on top of the mountain with no water; except for what we could carry. I have always considered myself quite the outdoorsman, hiker, backpacker, but I have to admit that this was a first.

We are currently over 10,000 feet above sea level and headed higher. Ninety miles into our trek, we are all sweating from our exertion that day. It seems as if we have been climbing all day. Crossing the last stream of the day, we debate exactly how much water we can carry on the last ascent of the day. Everyone fills their four one liter bottles and off we go. We literally can not carry anymore than this, since all of our bottles are now full.

For the first time in my life, I am going to spend 36 hours with only four liters of water. Wait a minute, why am I panicking, people live 4-5 days with zero water. I am only going to sleep. But, I have to hike this mountain, which will take at least two bottles. It is hot and I am sweating. I need to cook and clean for two meals and then hike down the other side before we will see water again. I like to sleep beside a rushing stream. Who made this plan? Who is putting us at the top of the mountain rather than the valley? I know who.

My life changed at this exact moment. This was only for one night. Water would be available on the other side of the mountain awaiting us upon our descent. There are people in this world, who deal with this thought everyday of their lives. They either have no source, or one requiring an extended walk, or their source is contaminated, or all of the above.

It is still amazing to me what our habits are, what we are accustomed to. We are such creatures of habit. We turn on our faucet and we get all the water we can possibly want, the average American family uses 175 gallons per day, and I was definitely an average American. For me personally, a few years ago upon moving into the mountains, the only source of drinking water was a well. But we have our own personal well, that is located just a few feet from our home. It pumps directly into the whole house filter system. No worries, right. Then the electricity goes out, presto no water. So, my mind had already begun a transformation, before that fateful climb up Mt. Phillips. It was open, shall we say, due an enlightening.

Back to the trek, the boys in our crew at Philmont were a bit confused. "We can't carry enough water to drink, cook, clean, and do all the things we normally do". Even if we do things the way we do them backpacking, which is a long way from "normal camping", there will not be enough water for the night. Agreed, not the way we do things with our current mindset, but what if we think differently now. We have no water or certainly a very limited amount of water.

Requiring the boys and leaders to think outside of the box was the quintessential task of this "dry camp". Having been an avid backpacker for almost thirty years, you camp near water, right? Why would you choose to camp away from water, to live away from water? Sometimes you have no choice. My boys, under my leadership, had no idea of how far I was personally out of my own comfort zone. What can you do differently? How can you conserve water? Can you do with less water? Certainly you can! You simply adjust your routine, habits, and your thought processes. I began to think of doing things one-step different or one step better. For years, while learning "leave no trace" principles, it was all about leaving a camp site better than you found it. My granddaddy told stories of how he would clean a public bathroom. He would actually take two seconds and wipe down a counter with his towel That was the norm. You would not dare leave a bathroom counter dirty for the next person. Wow, what if everyone took one more step in their lives to make things one step better, to leave things better than they found them.

It was very basic concept, actually. But was it really that simple? For us, we ate lunch and snack foods for our evening meal, thus requiring no cooking or cleaning water. We drank what we needed and all laughed the next day at how we had "survived". But, things were different now; at least for me. I would never view water the same. My life had changed. Things were beginning to surface from where they had been placed years ago.

Please look for **Soul Water** soon, where you find **Soul Grub**.

Soul Water

By: Tom Roberson
Soul Dreams Publishing
P. O. Box 153
Talking Rock, GA 30175

www.soul-dreams.com

PRE- ORDER

Pre-Order copies of **Soul Water** now.

Send check or money order along with order form below to:

Soul-Dreams Publishing
P. O. Box 153
Talking Rock, GA 30175

OR

Order online

www.soul-dreams.com

sales @soul-dreams.com

Please send me _____ copies of **Soul Water** at $14.95 each, plus $2.50 shipping and handling per book ordered.

Mail books to :

Name _____
Address _____
City _____
State _____
Zip _____
Email _____

Tom Roberson

Over the course of his lifetime, **Tom Roberson** has dedicated much of his volunteer hours to the youth of his community. Many different sports dominated the horizon in the early years, baseball, soccer, cross country, and track; however, water skiing was always the underlying focus. Watching his boys and daughter earn their ways to National rankings and titles, was the pinnacle of a dream that he had for himself many years earlier. But, not only did he see his children accomplish so much; he watched many other children and adults achieve goals they never thought reachable.

As with so many of his lifelong ventures, **Tom** worked many hours with his children to achieve these titles and goals. Many mornings were spent at the dock teaching and training. Many afternoons were spent on the soccer field. But, the same has rang true with his professional endeavors. Many cups of coffee have been shared to close the deal or make the sale. And, when you talk about the numbers of miles trekked, paddled, and camped, with many young men that learned life long lessons, you might say **Tom** was and always will be a "boy at heart.", most certainly a Boy Scout at heart. Maybe this is why his passion for youth continues to run strong today.

It was ultimately the time spent as a Scout Leader, that created the fondest memories. All the while, the boys thought they were doing all of the learning and growing, they had no idea of the transformation that there old Scout leader was going through. Not only have his passions and desires changed in this life, but he has been challenged to do many things he never thought possible. All the while pushing people to do things they never thought possible.

This book is the first in a series sharing some of the things in his heart. We are starting with the food, because everyone knows the way to a man's heart is through his stomach. Next up, will be **Soul Water**, soon to be followed by **Soul Searchin'**.